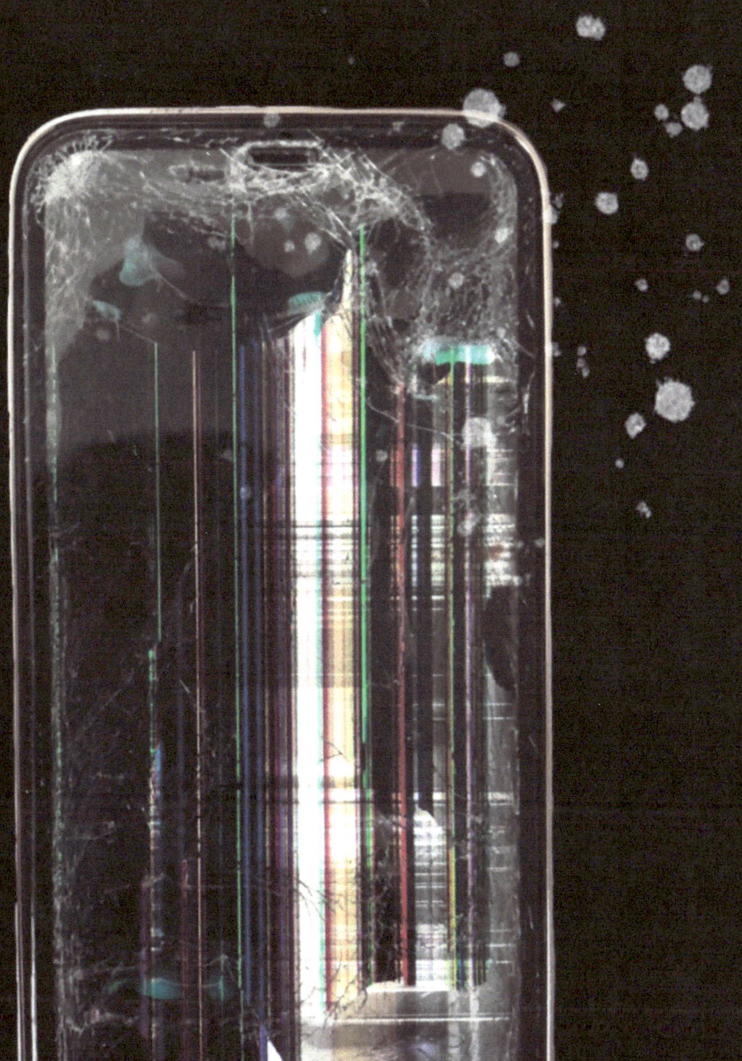

Insta Face

Insta Face

This art book is a commentary on the pretentious use of social media and the ever growing self image obsession of selfie culture. The worlds history transcends any amount of likes on the gram or does it? It appears nowadays that the worth of culture and our happiness is reduced to aesthetics and likes. FOMO reducing people further to usefulness and productivity.

Is the colosseum worth visiting unless it has your perfectly 3d printed symmetrical face next to it? The perfect picturesque wedding proposal in front of the colosseum is ironic. The copy and paste of modern romanticism is competing over virtual induced serotonin. And I wonder who started the trend of posing in-front on a death theatre to represent love.

Is love not enough anymore do we need to be in front of a famous city monument to prove to strangers that love is real. That we are successful. That we are worth life. Because someone else who we don't know or probably wouldn't even like has rated us. The heart emoji a representation of modern cheaply bought love.

In truth to the narcissistic portrayal of the self from the personal gaze online I have used my own selfies. As well as the cost of living crisis availability of my own face. It reflects modern life. I utilised the free apps to add layers of filters, effects, photoediting and collage. The images are not the typical perfection seen online. I have used the technology to create demonic and dark feminine alter egos. Many based on mythology such as gorgons. Inspired by myths of beautiful women turned monstrous due to envy, pain and lust. This satire work developed from the way women who are not pure and obedient are portrayed in art and literature as demonic. Instead of the typical portrayal of soft, sexual use of filters and editing to create perfect avatar women.

My work explores how filters can be used to edited our looks in to multiple versatile ways to something far beyond humanity and beauty. How true beauty is often hidden and even more so in a world that shuns anything that doesn't conform to social standards. Even when the standards withheld are unbearable and steals free will. With so many choices available for women to cheaply invest and enhance themselves externally, upgrade the body work like a car. The modern women is obliged to turn into a mass produced product. Appearance is what a women's success have been held too. And looks appear to be even more important for survival than ever before. With academia especially in the arts being called a corpse now women and the marginalised showed up. The self image has become a product and the internet an accessible sales platform for all, so why not ? Women can take there own self image into thier own hands. This is my direct gaze of the artistic use of filters and self image as a woman that lives in the 21st century.

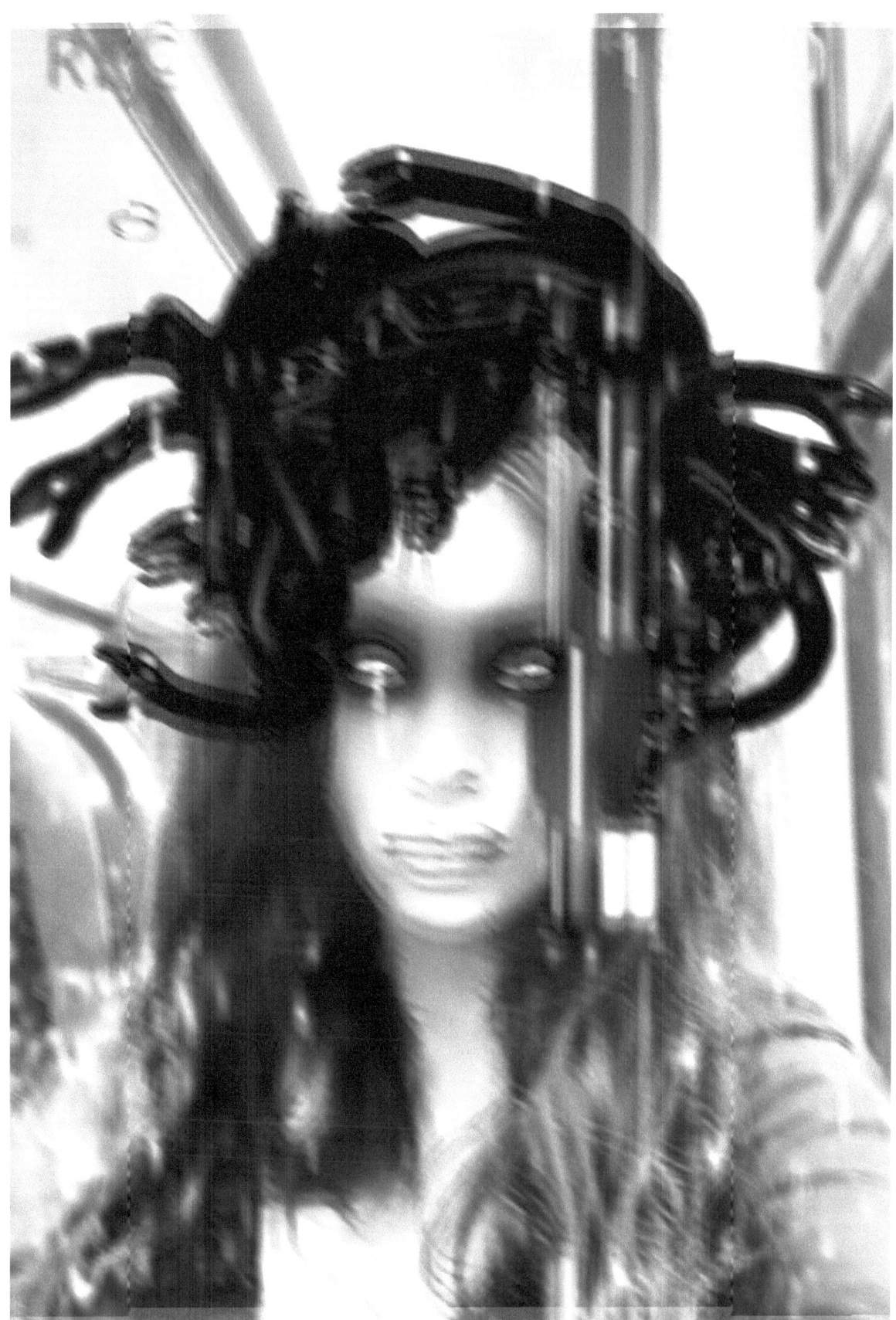

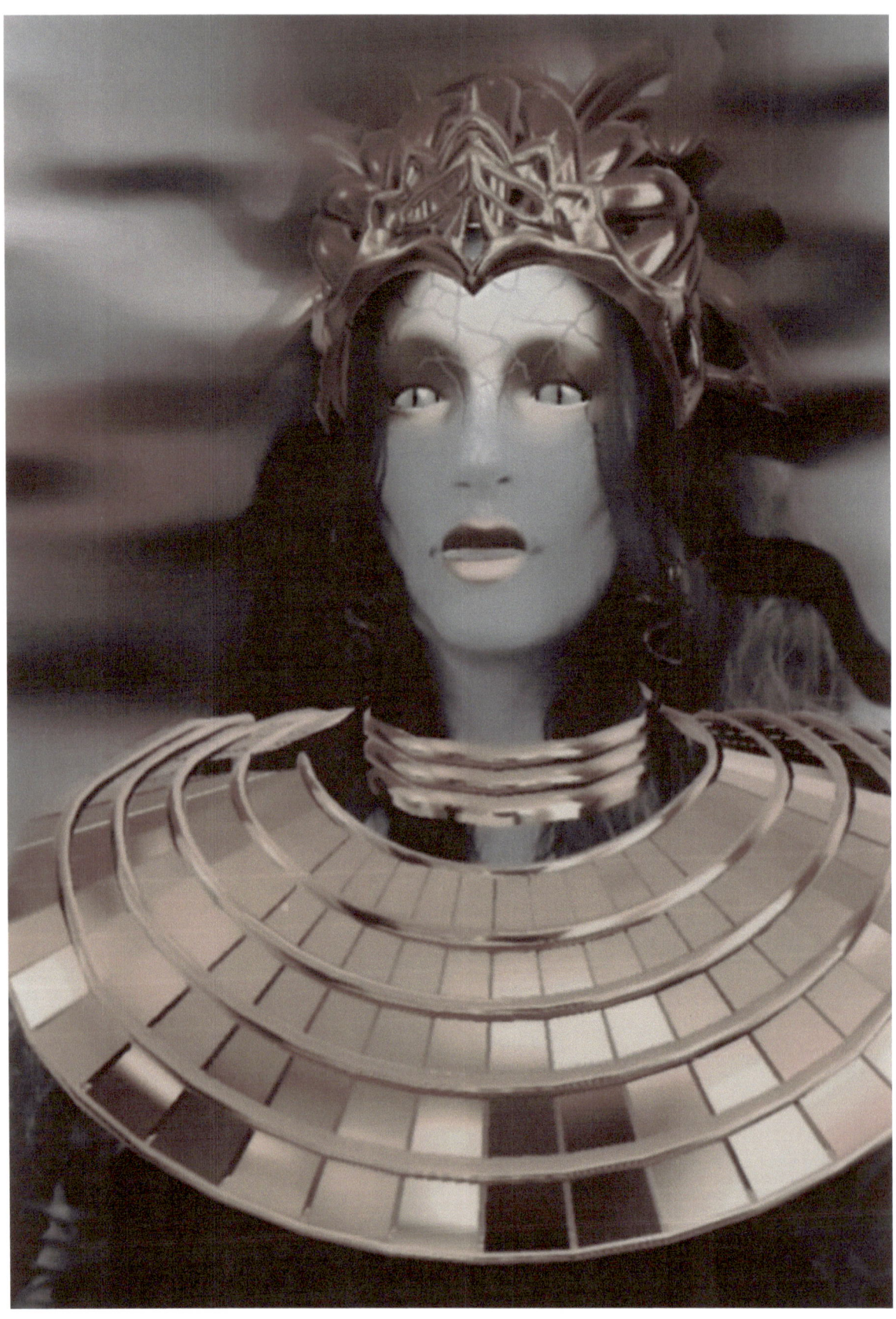

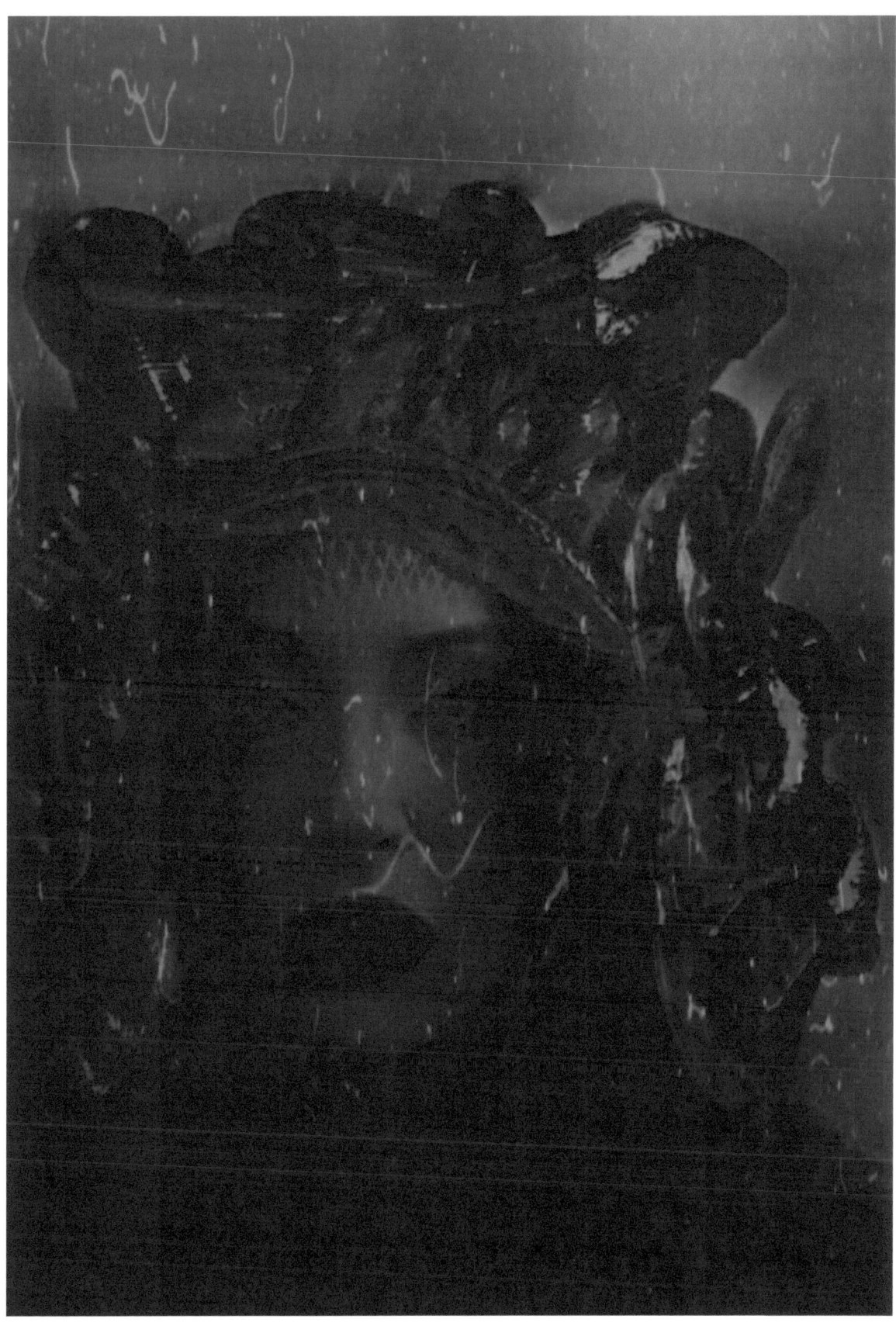

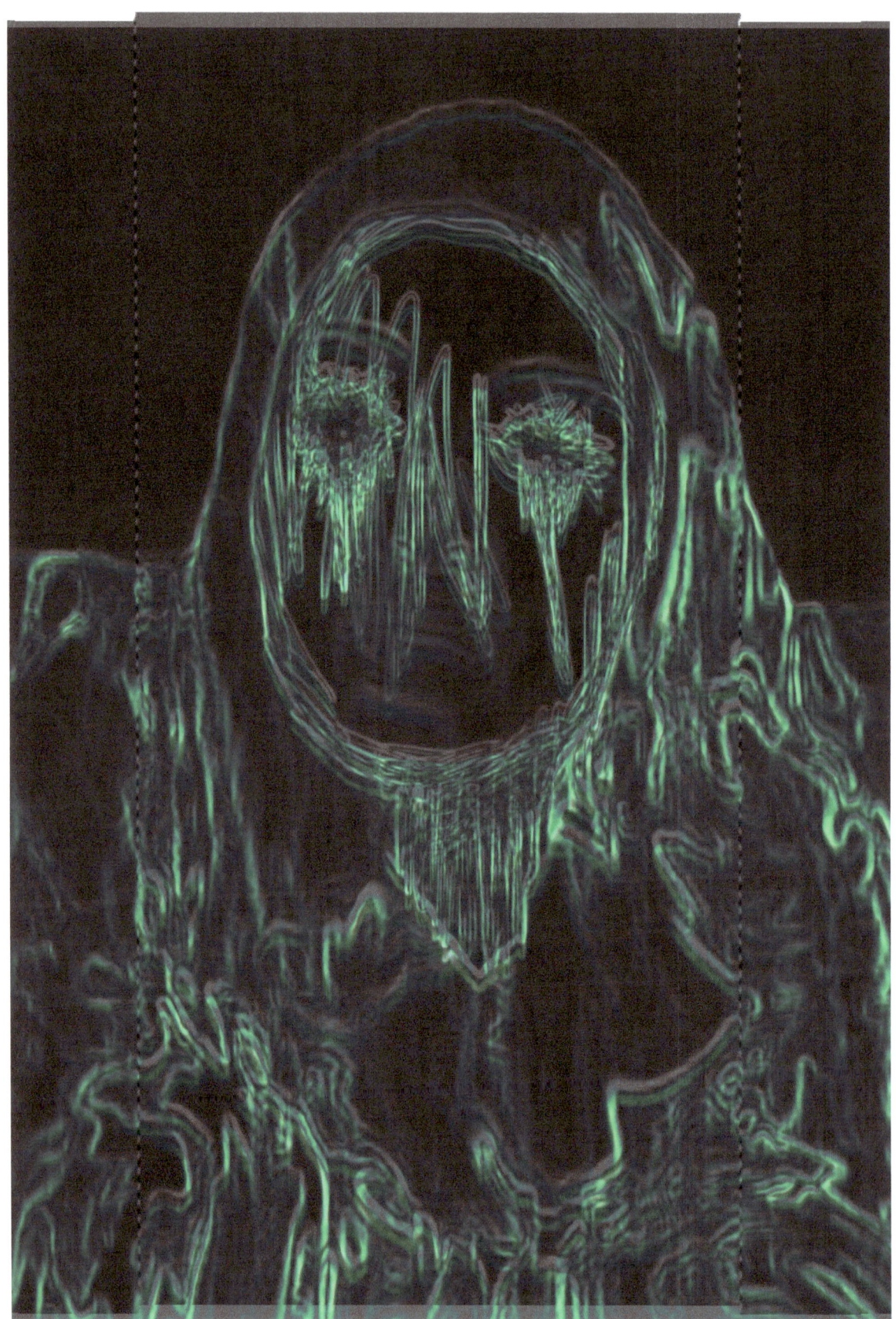

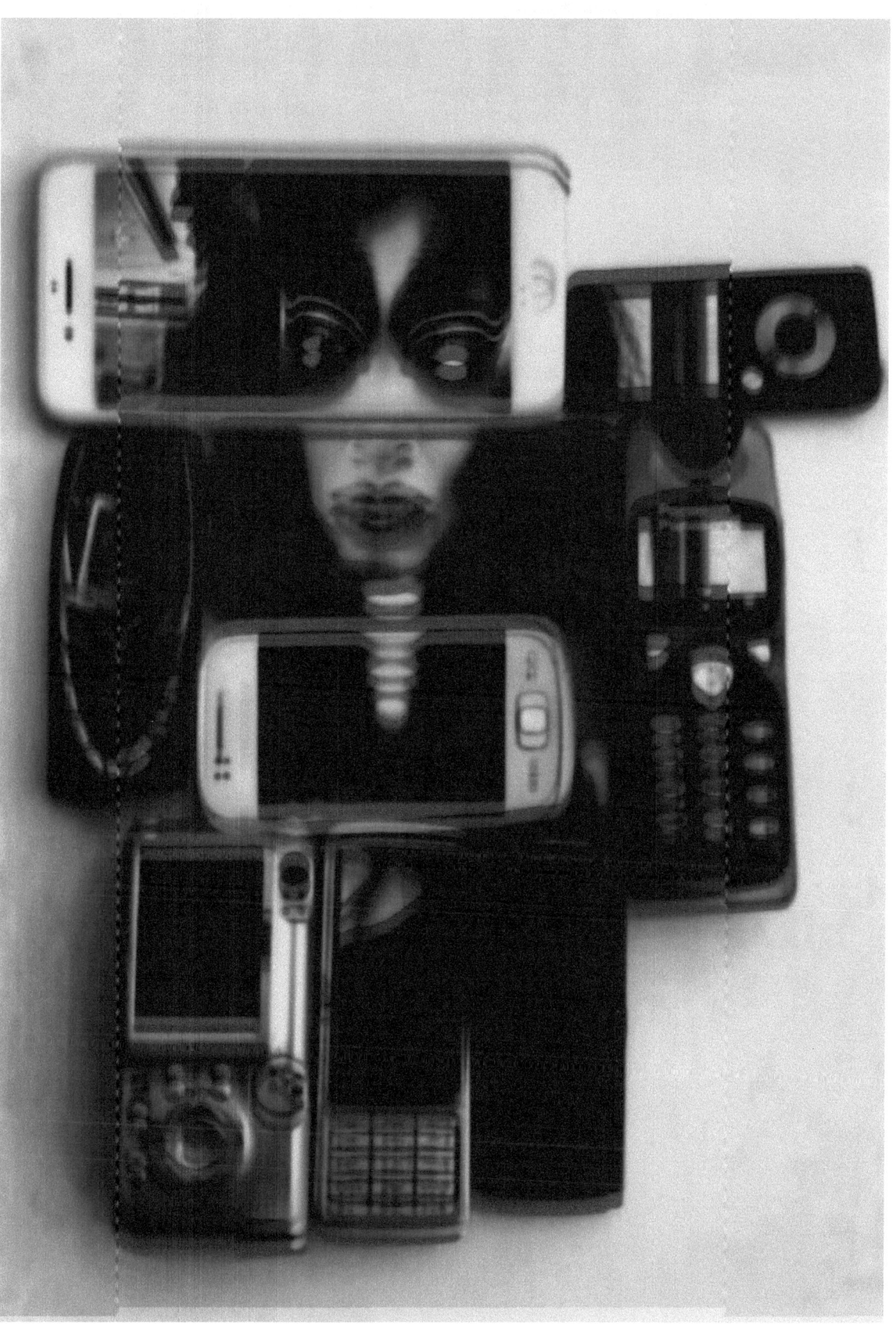

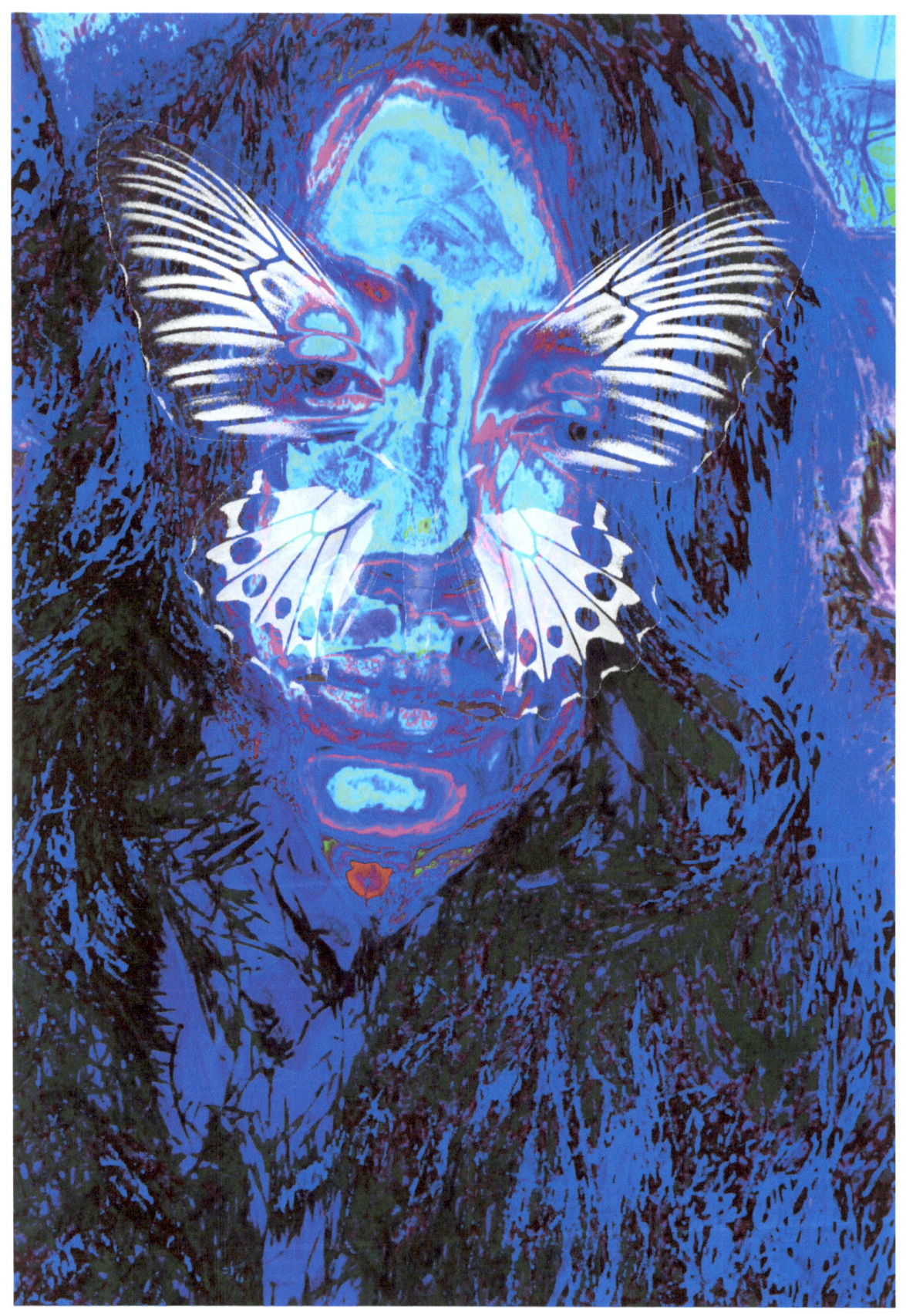

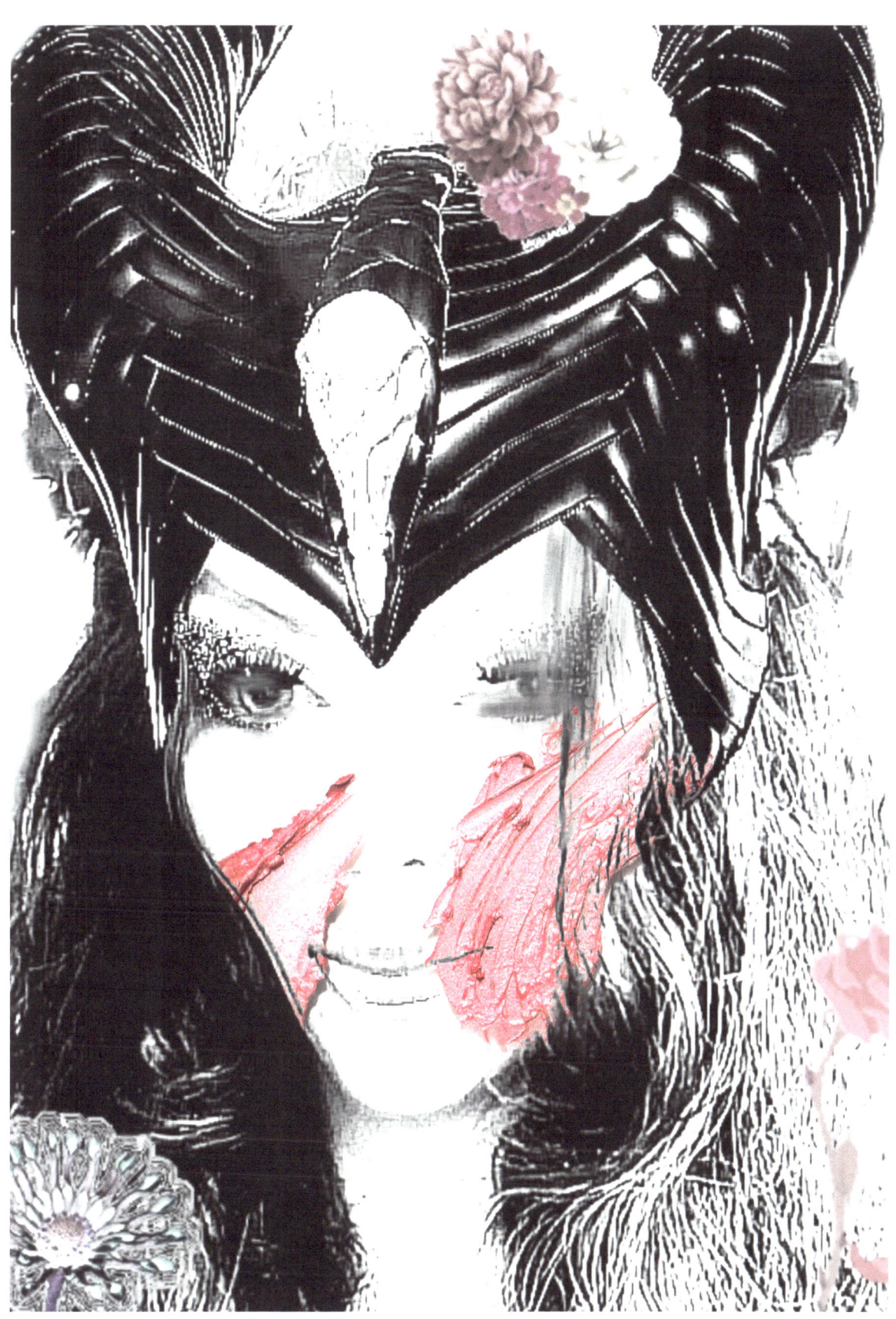

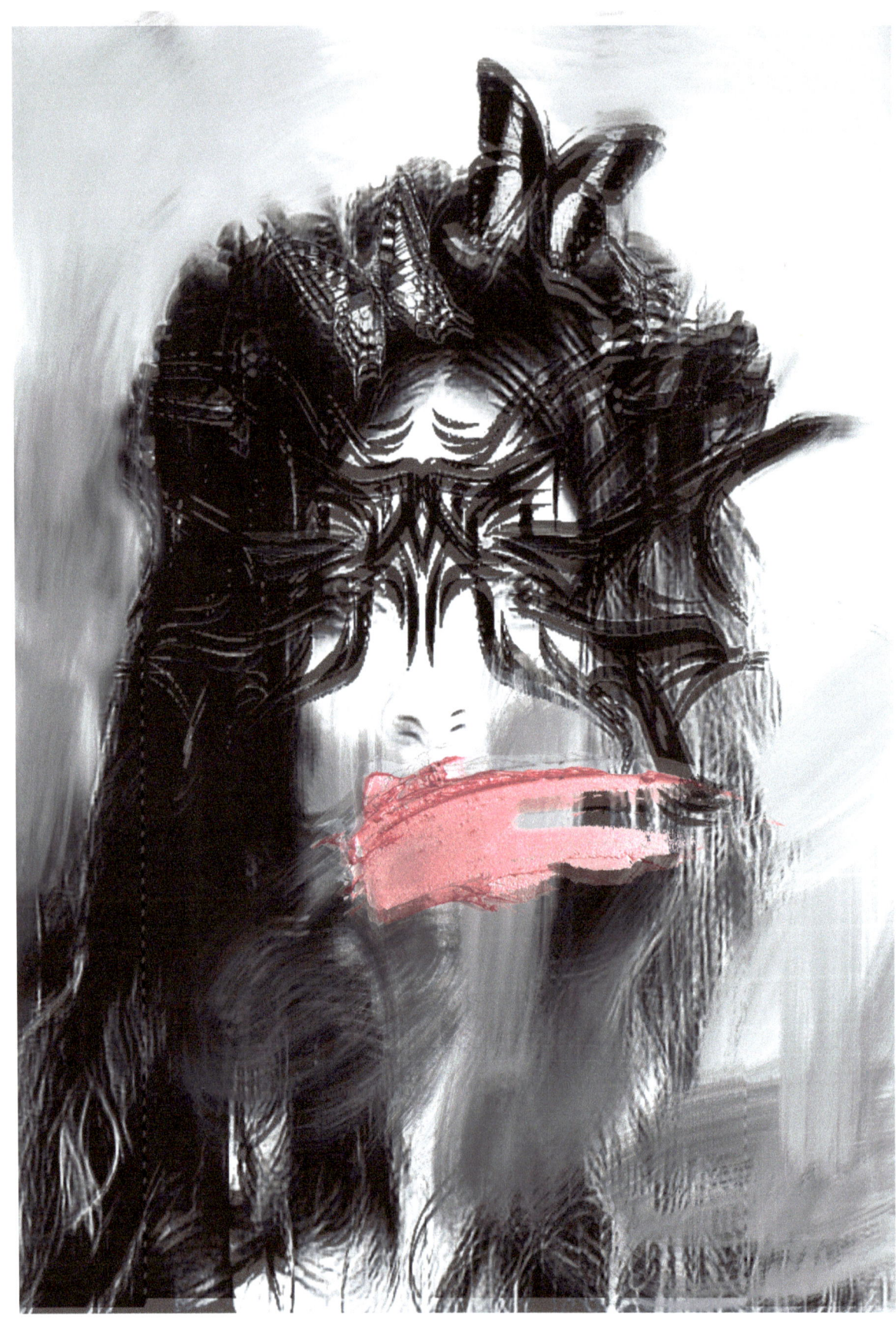

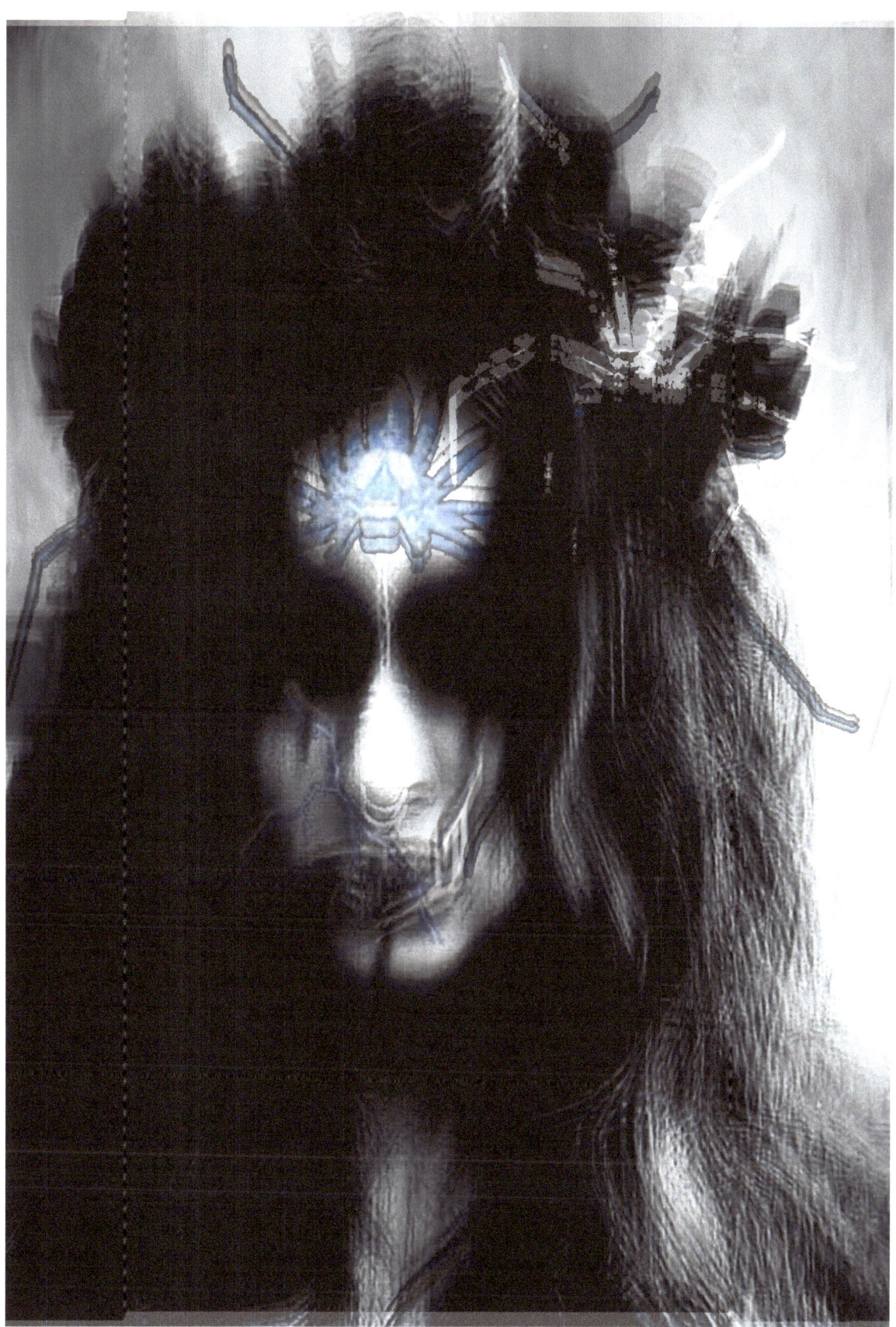

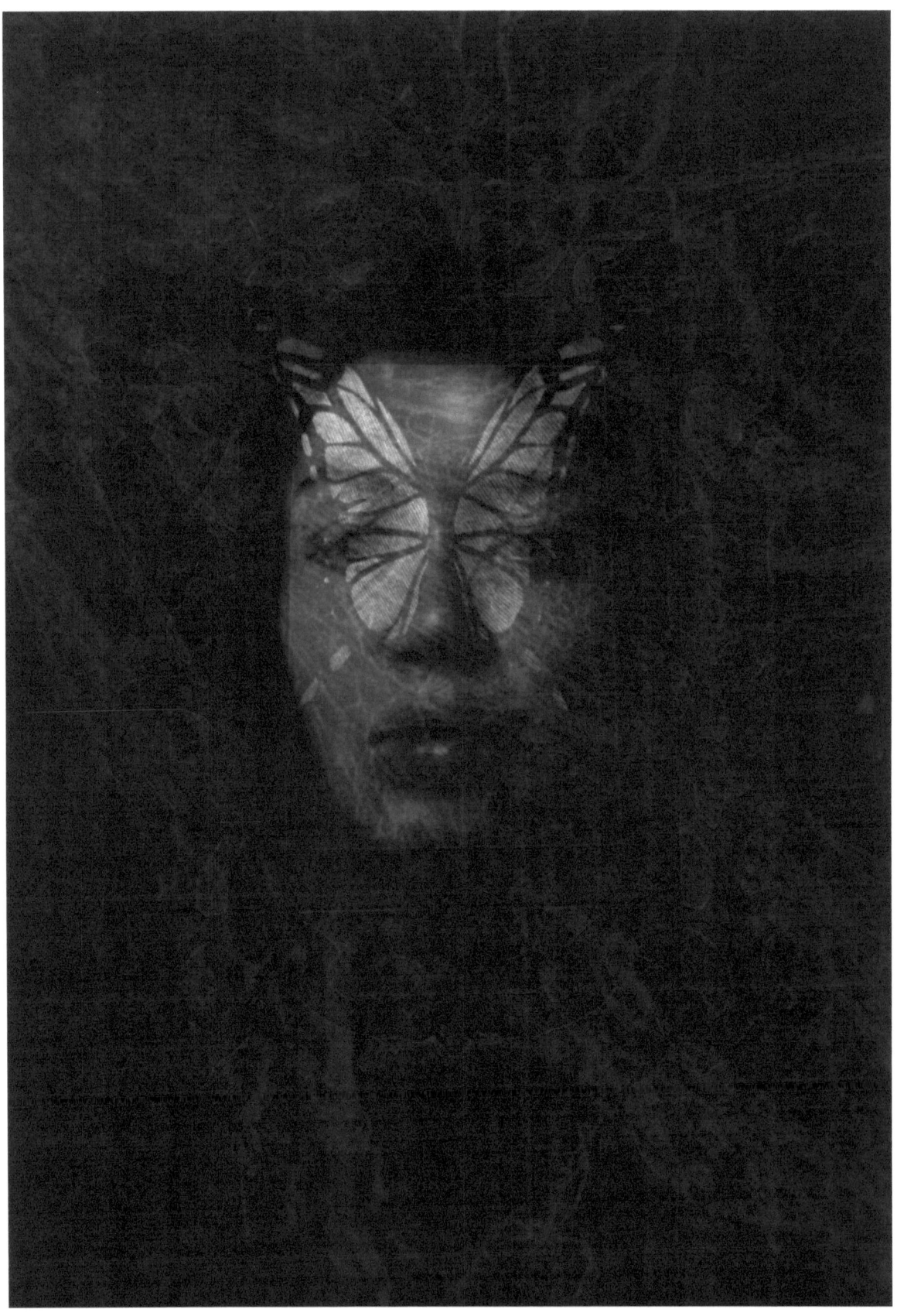

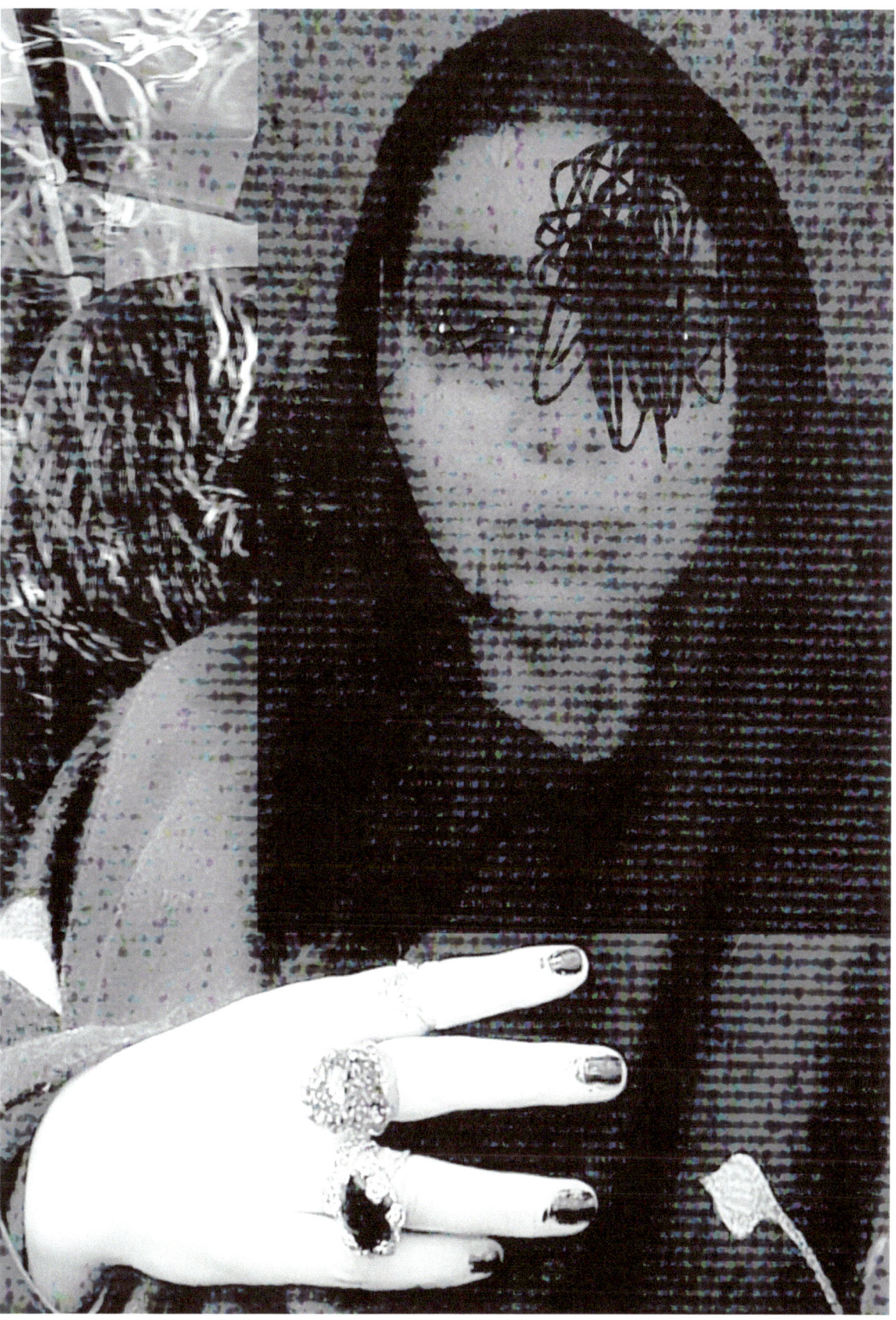

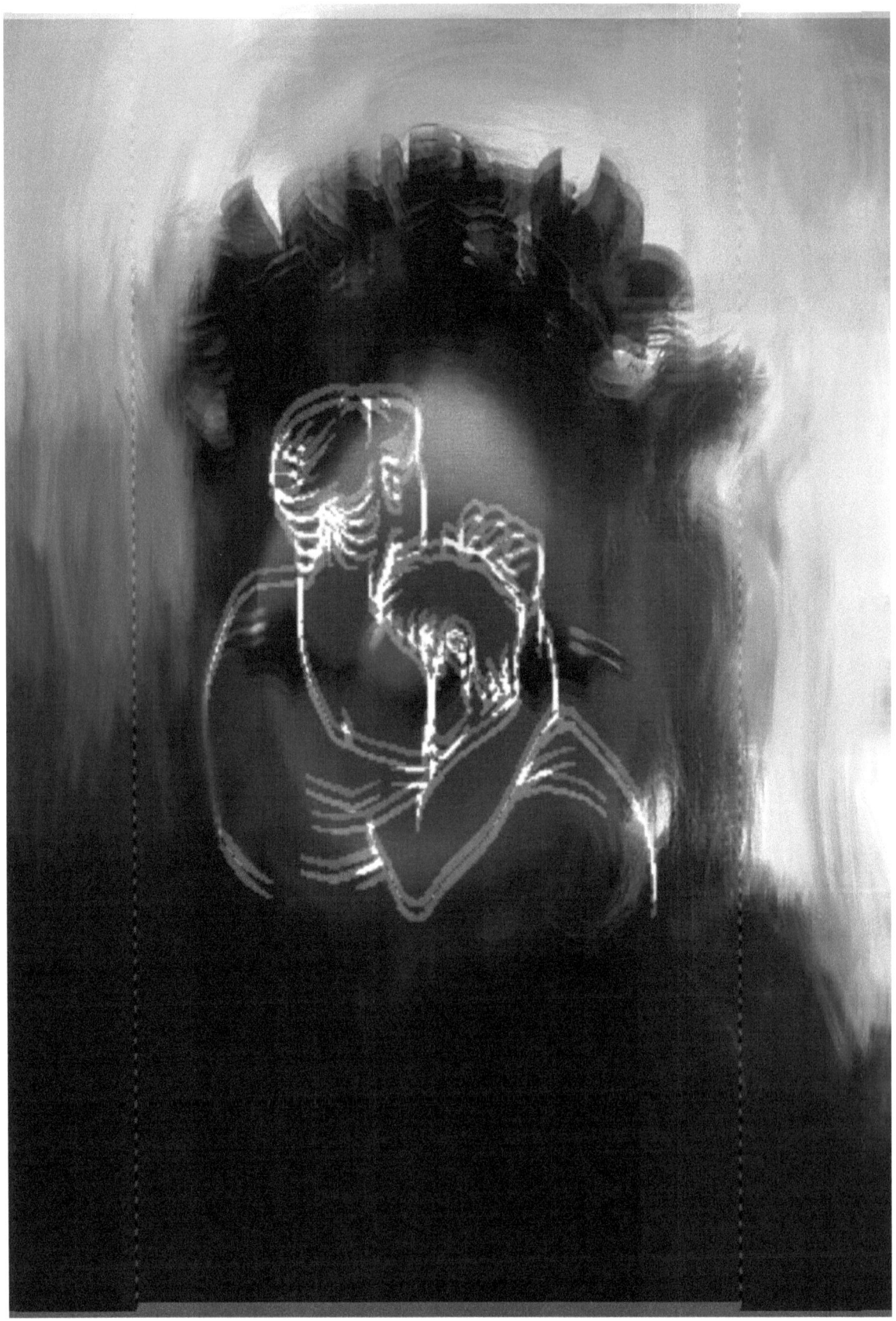

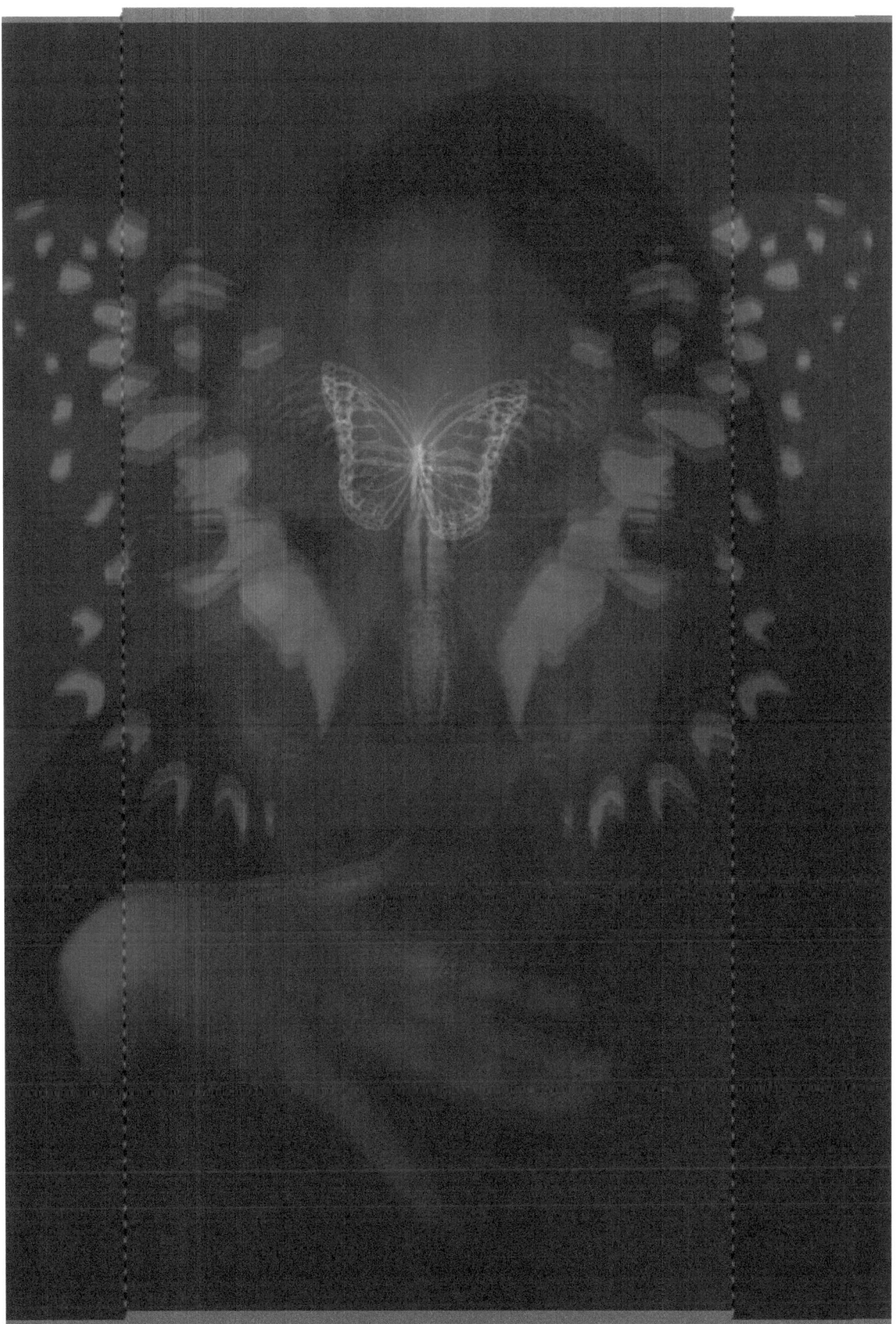

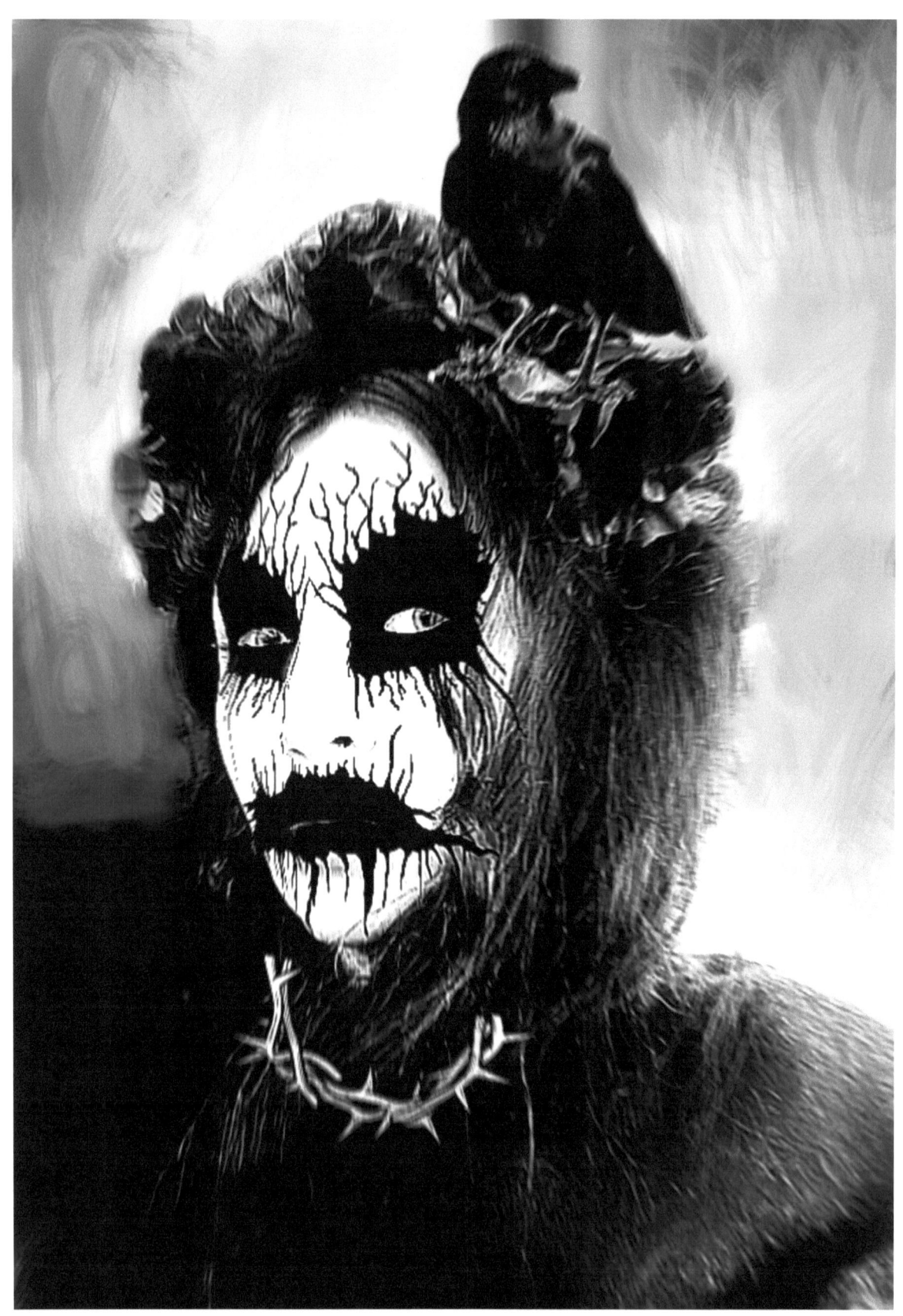

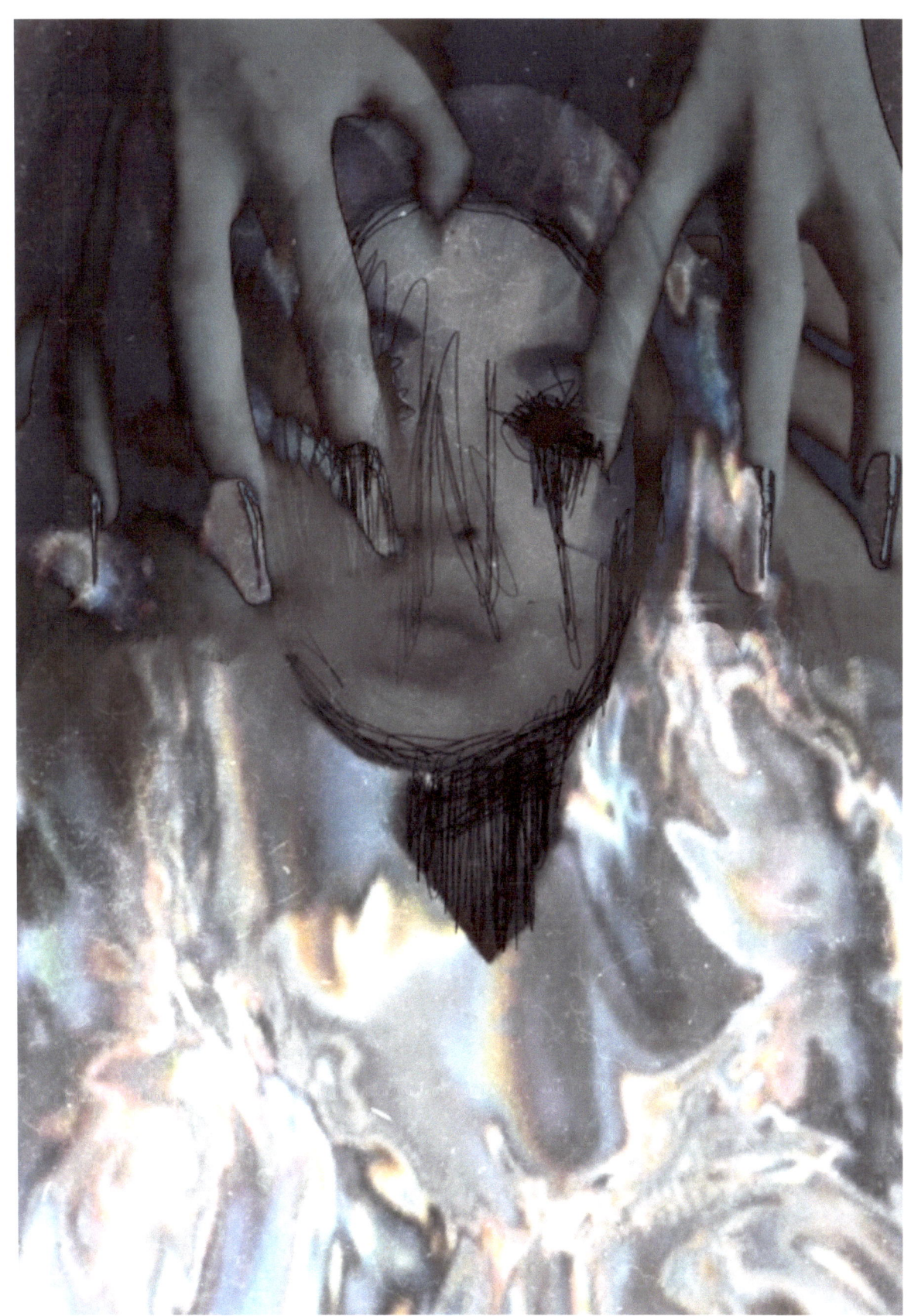

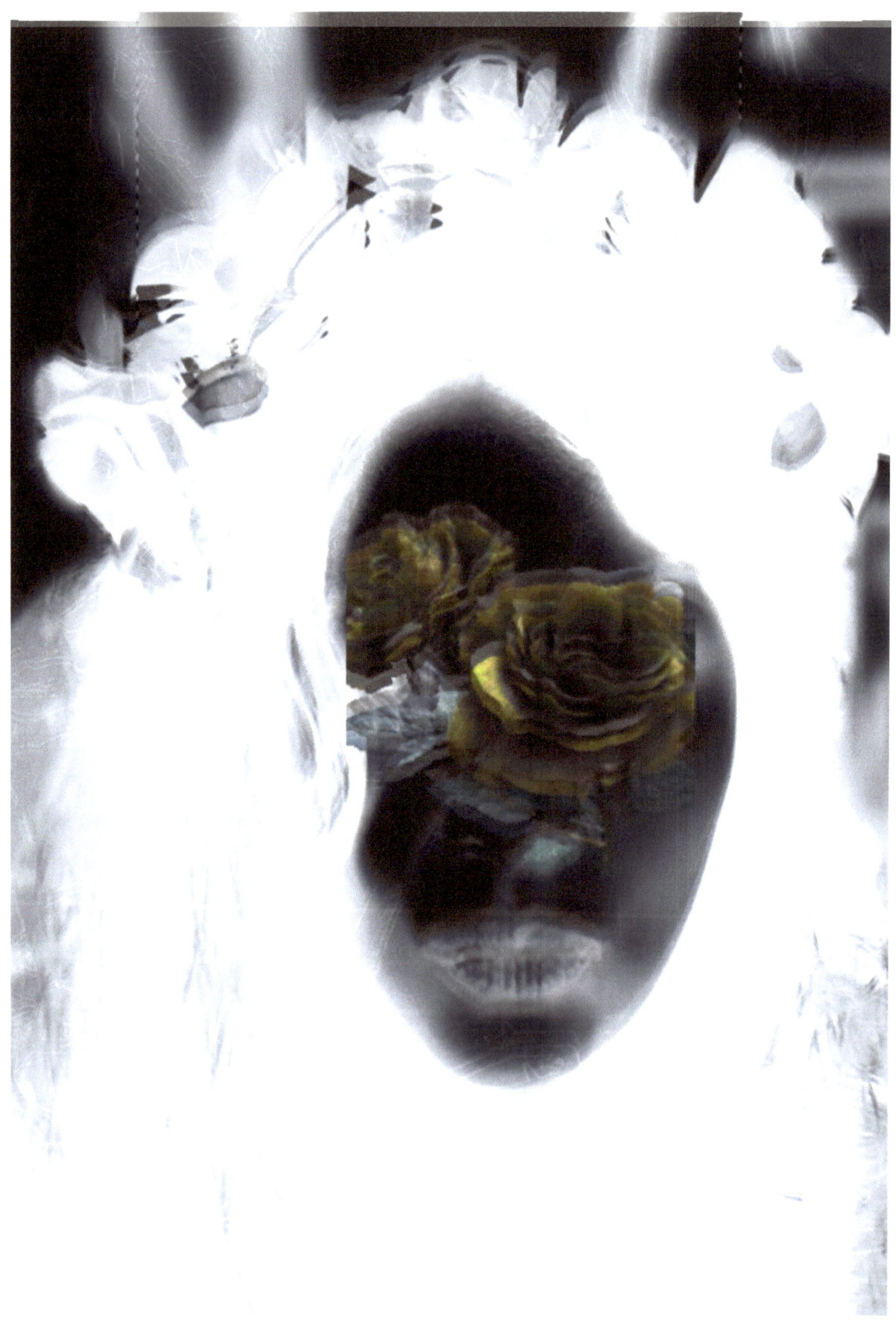

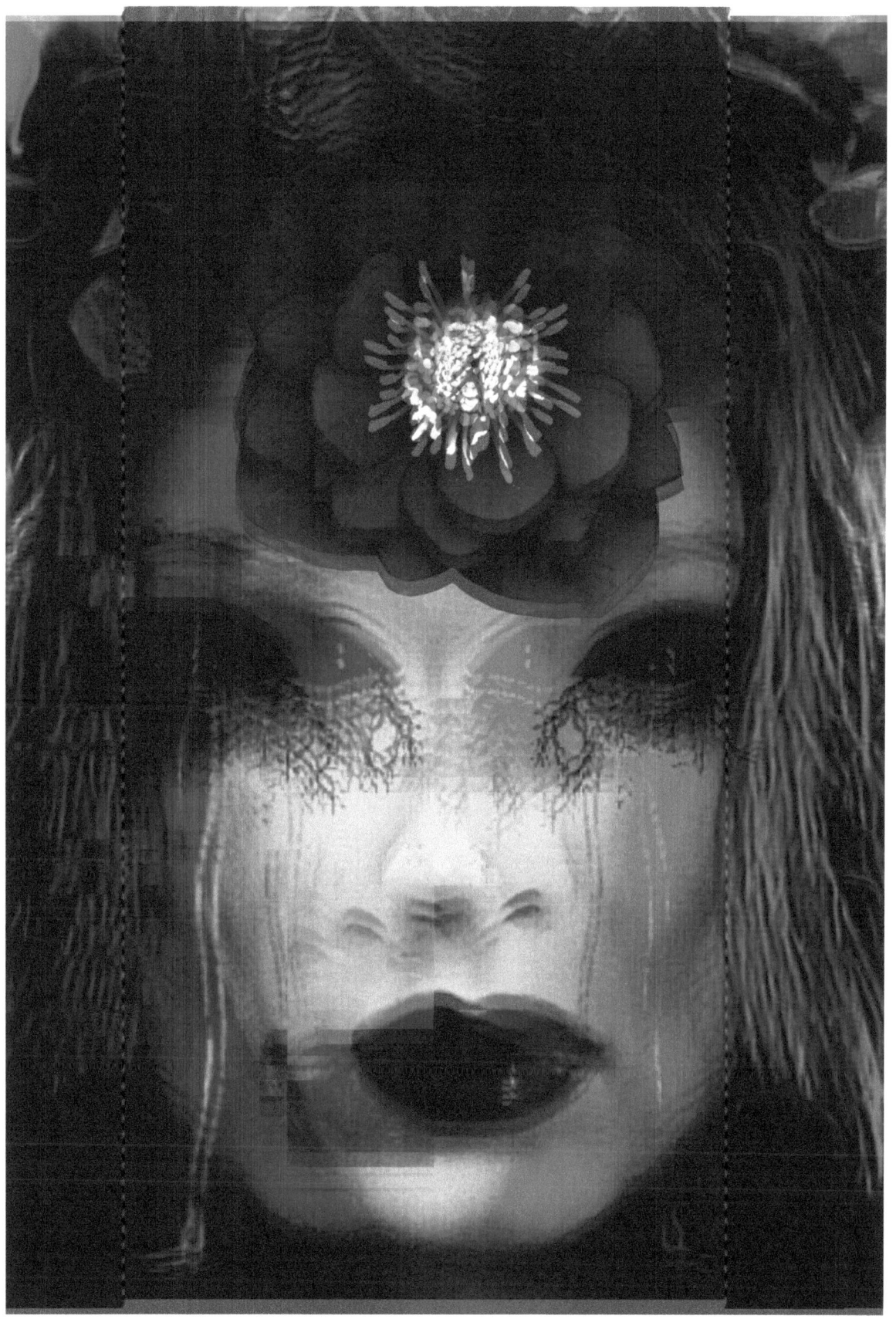

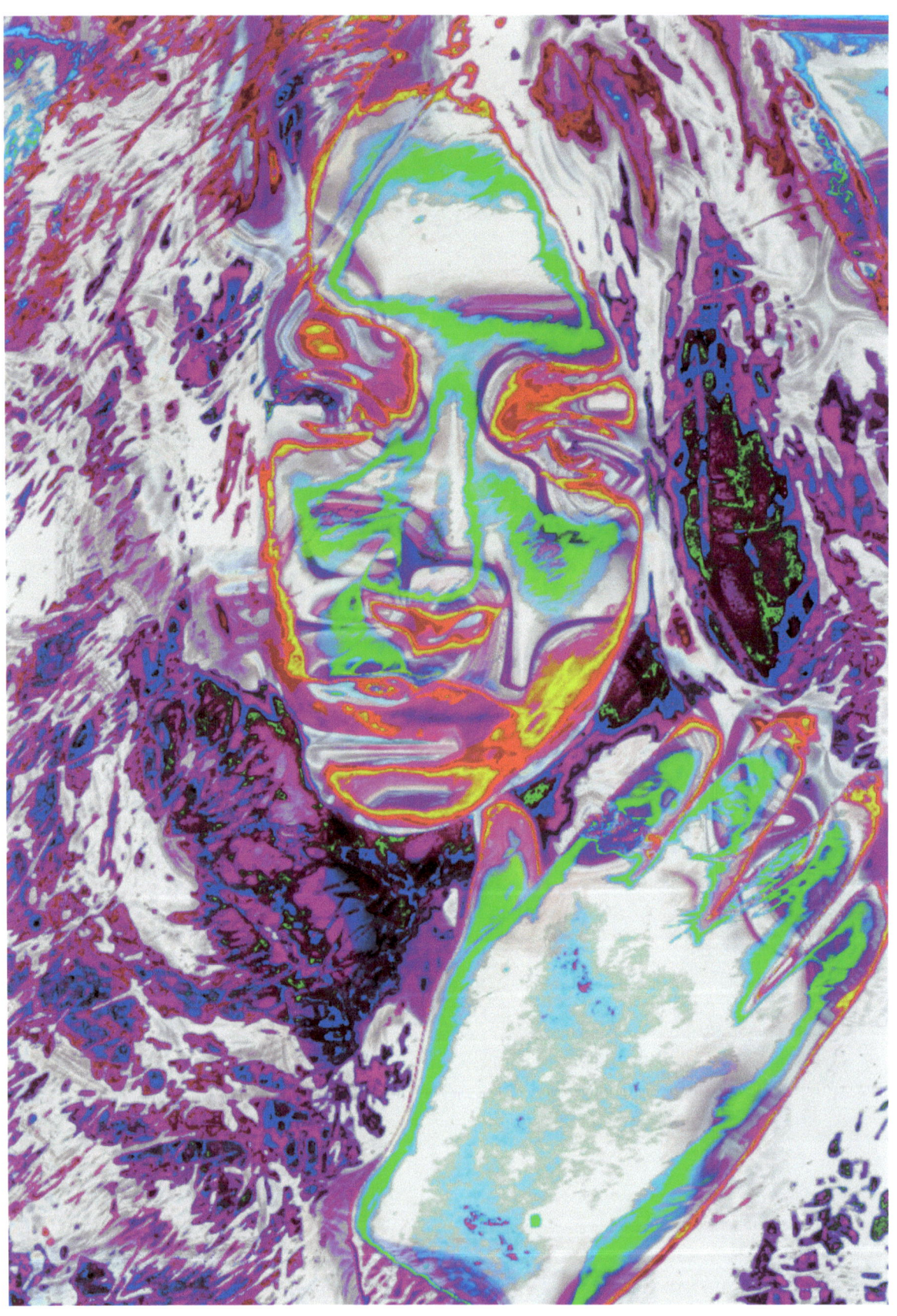

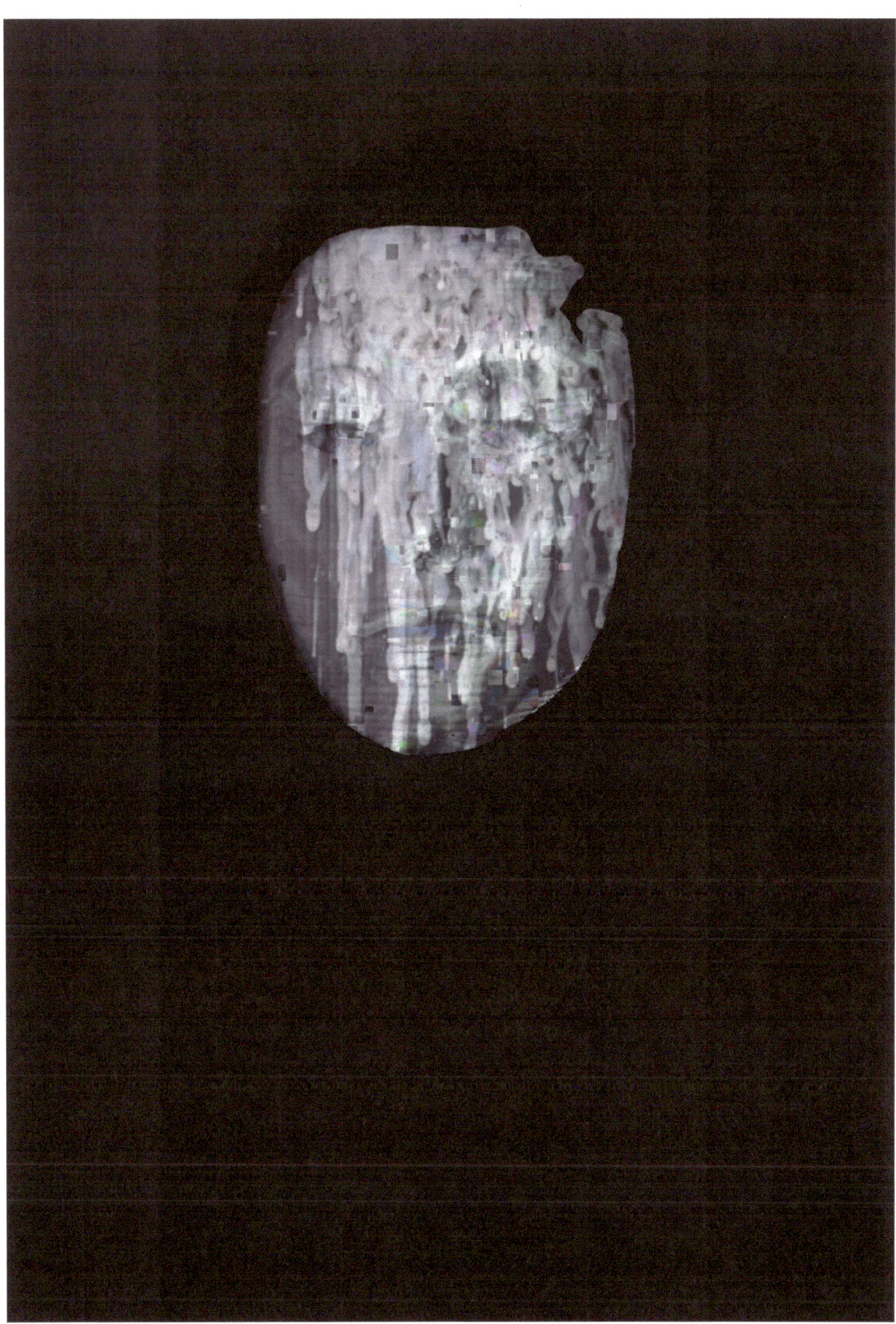

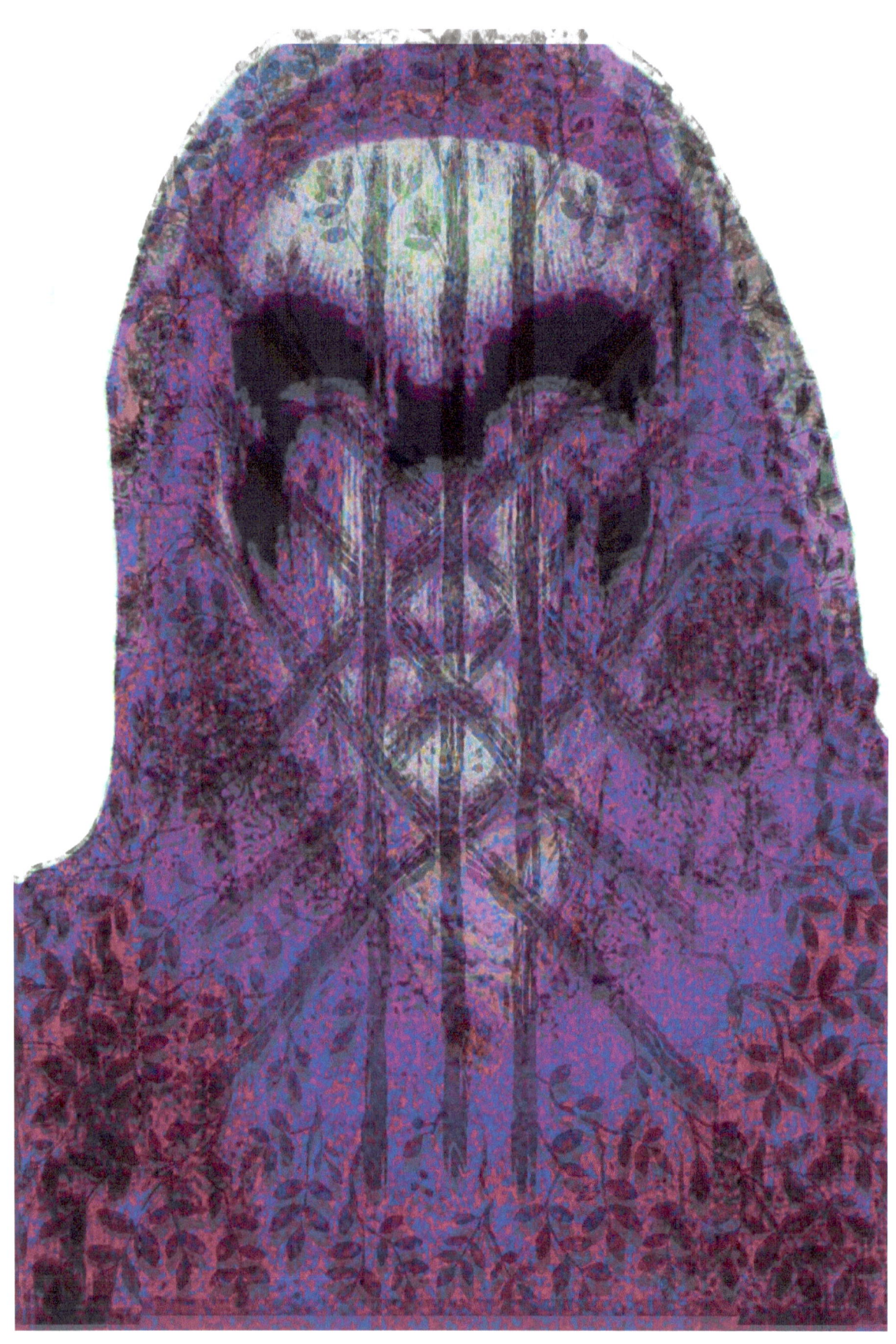

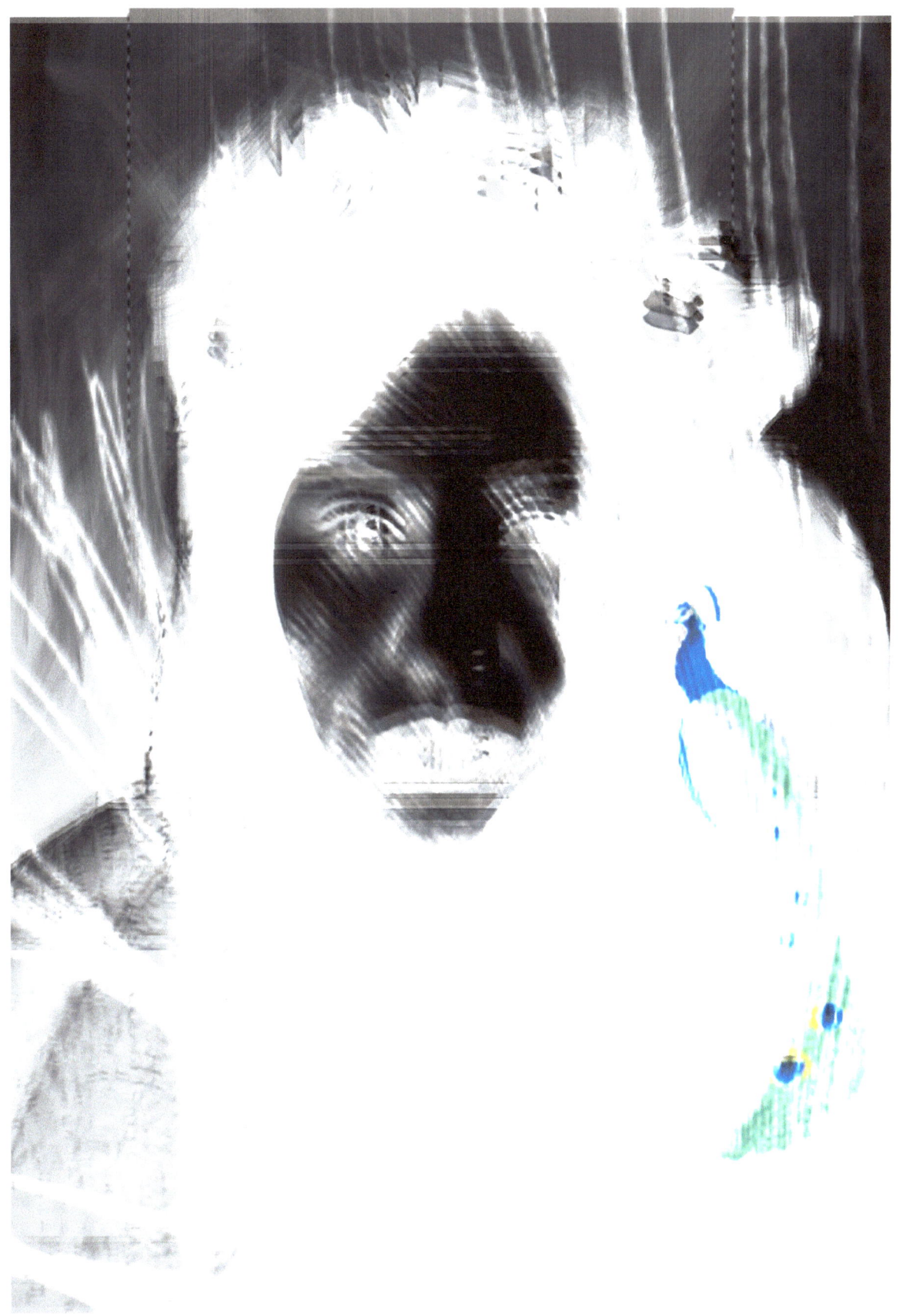

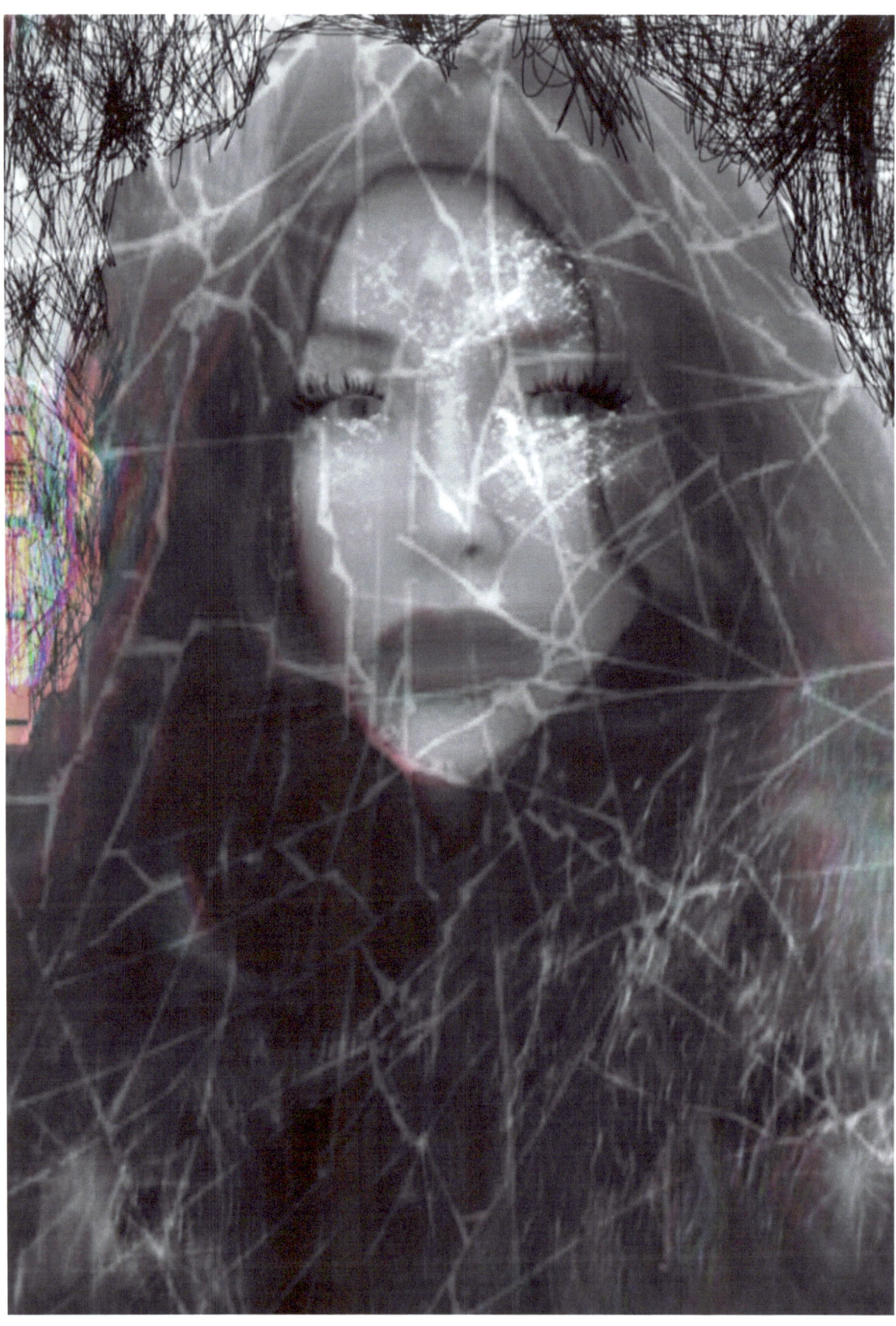

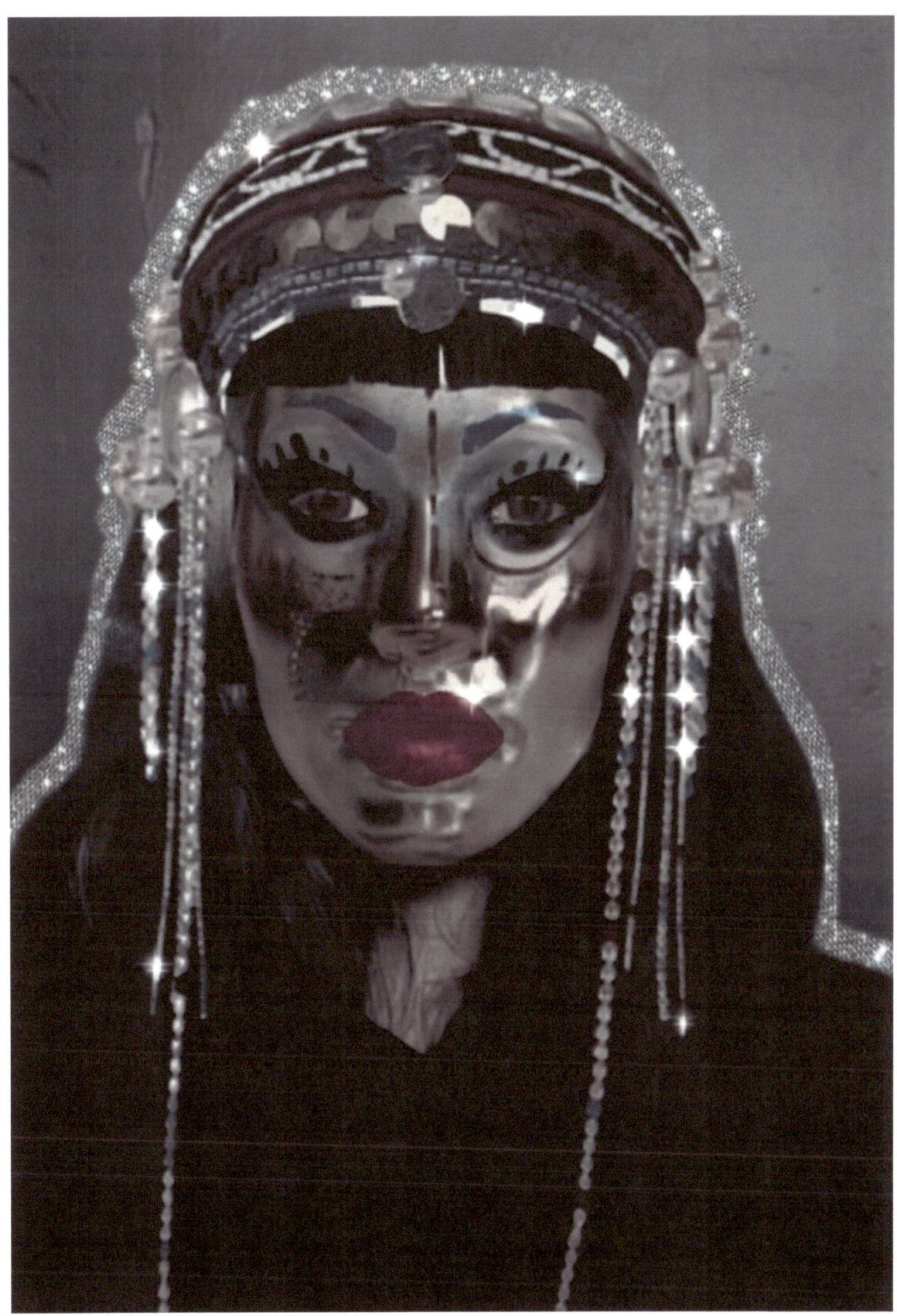

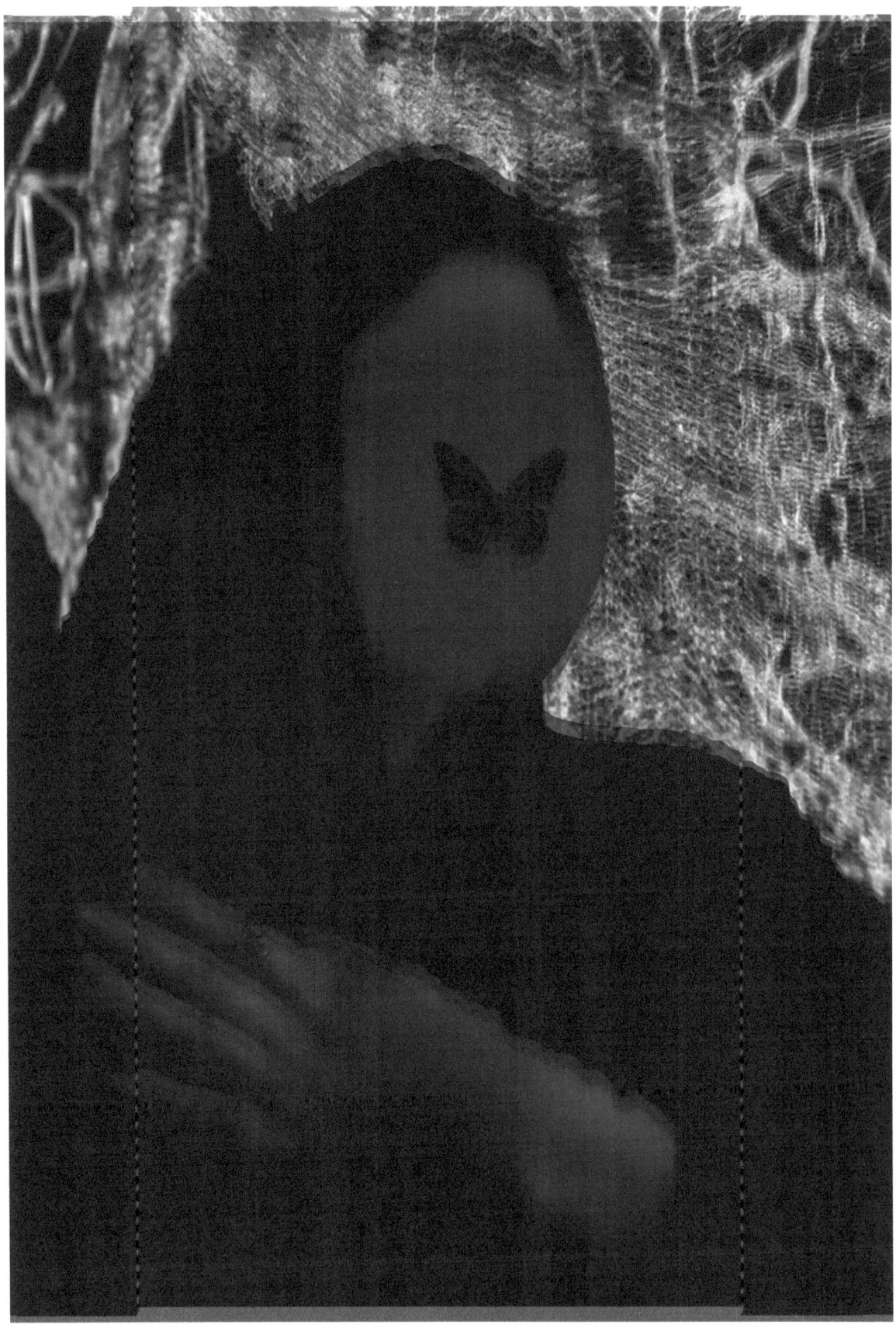

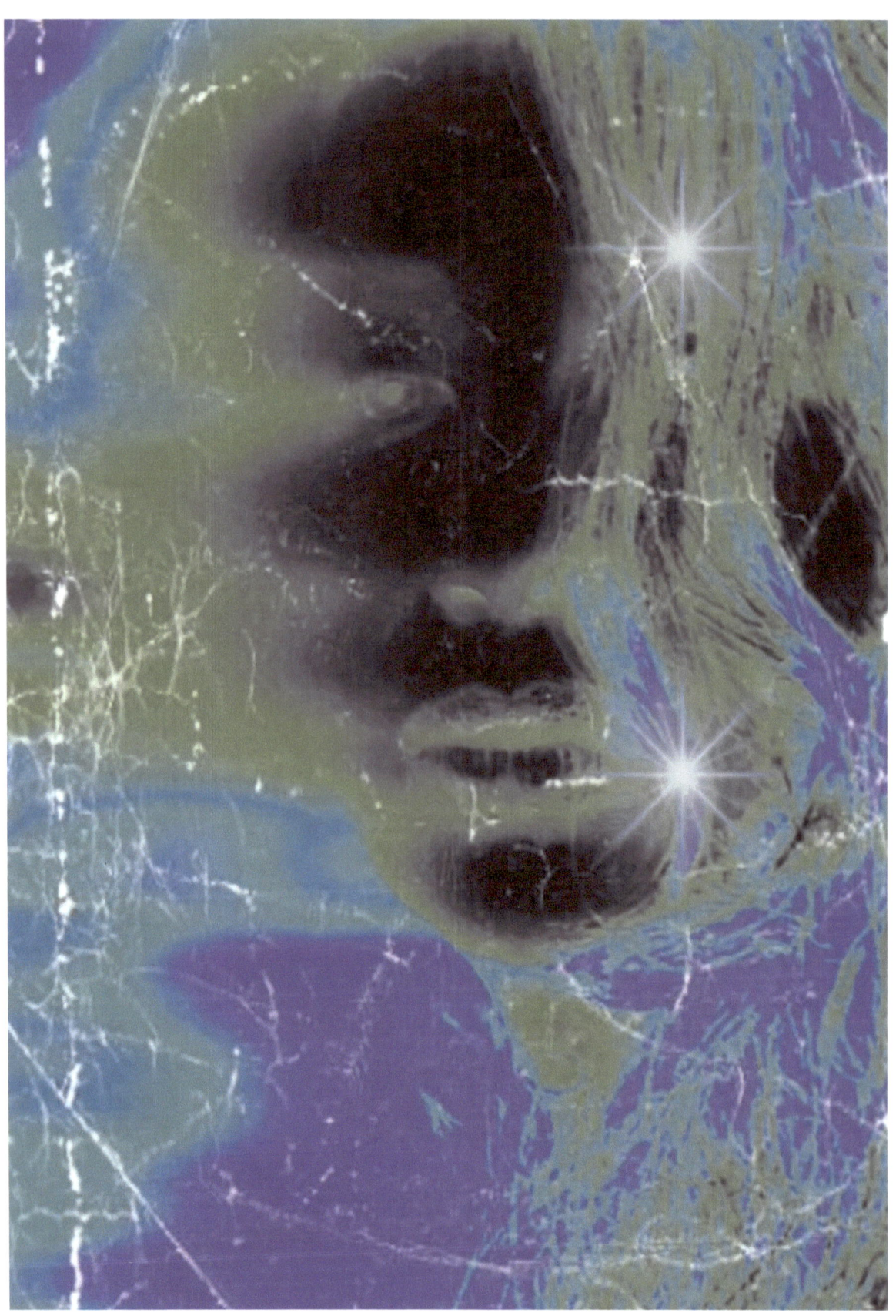

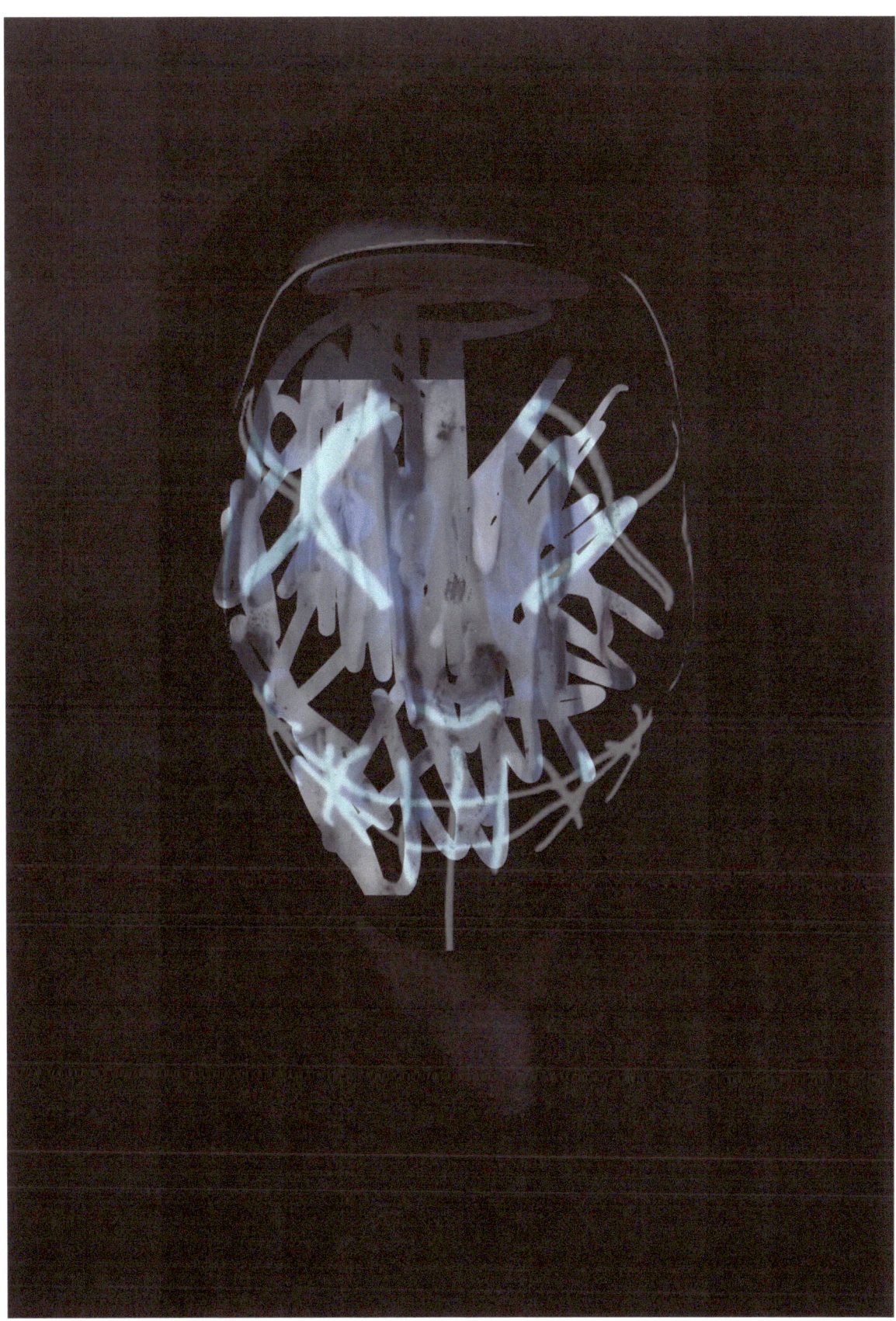

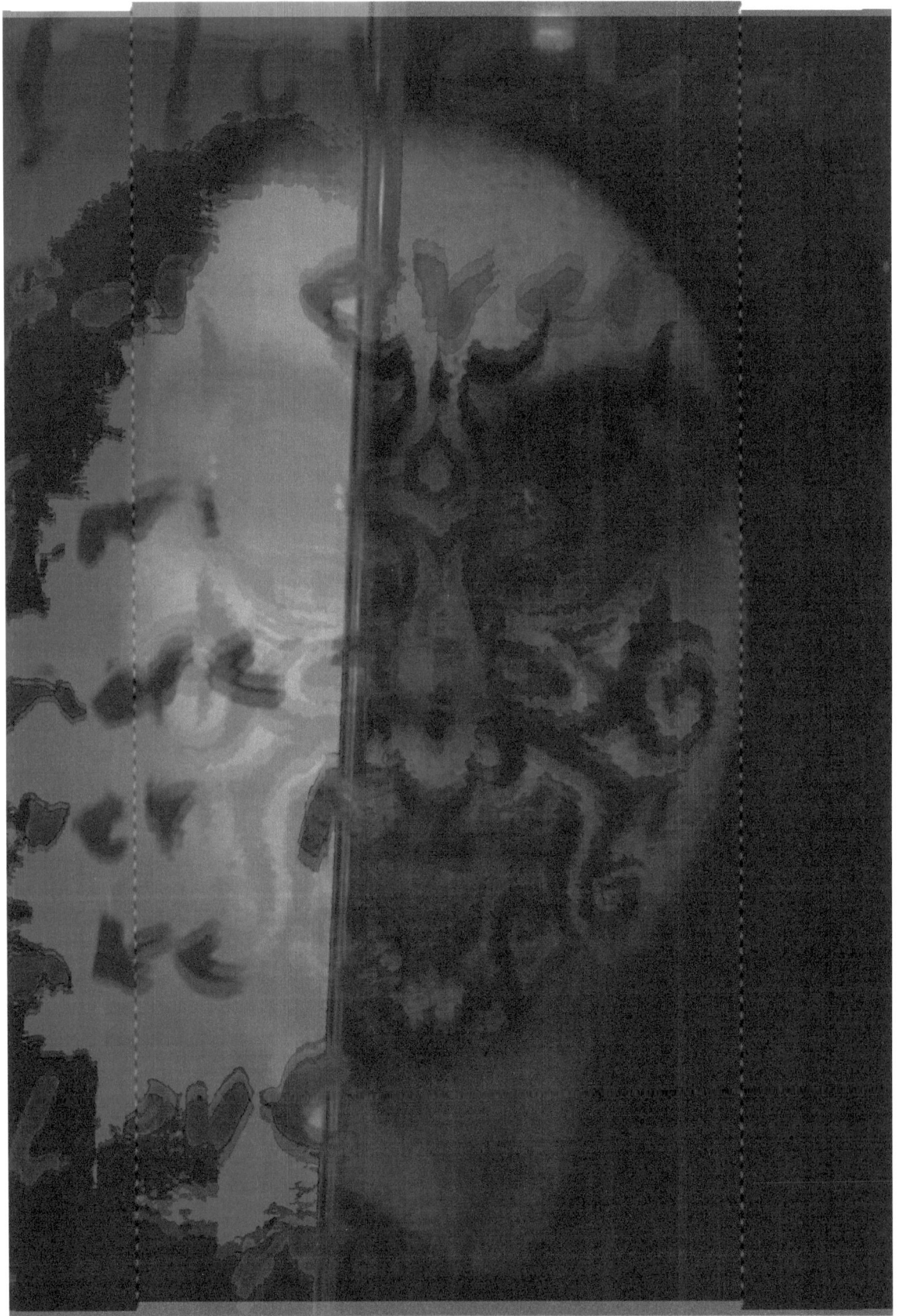